Fact Finders

PERSPECTIVES on HISTORY

JOHN BROWN

DEFENDING THE INNOCENT OR PLOTTING TERROR?

by Nel Yomtov

Consultant:
Richard Bell
Associate Professor of History
University of Maryland, College Park

CAPSTONE PRESS
a capstone imprint

Fact Finders Books are published by Capstone Press,
1710 Roe Crest Drive, North Mankato, Minnesota 56003
www.capstonepub.com

Copyright © 2014 by Capstone Press, a Capstone imprint. All rights reserved. No part of this publication may be reproduced in whole or in part, or stored in a retrieval system, or transmitted in any form or by any means, electronic, mechanical, photocopying, recording, or otherwise, without written permission of the publisher.

Library of Congress Cataloging-in-Publication Data
Yomtov, Nel.
John Brown : defending the innocent or plotting terror? / by Nel Yomtov.
pages cm. — (Fact finders. Perspectives on History.)
Includes bibliographical references and index.
Summary: "Describes John Brown's actions leading up to, during, and after his raid on Harpers Ferry"— Provided by publisher.
ISBN 978-1-4765-0244-1 (library binding)
ISBN 978-1-4765-3408-4 (paperback)
ISBN 978-1-4765-3416-9 (ebook PDF)
1. Brown, John, 1800–1859—Juvenile literature. 2. Harpers Ferry (W. Va.)—History—John Brown's Raid, 1859—Juvenile literature. 3. Antislavery movements—United States—History—19th century—Juvenile literature. 4. Abolitionists—United States—Biography—Juvenile literature. I. Title.
E451.Y66 2014
973.7'116—dc23   2013001323

Editorial Credits
Mari Bolte, editor; Ted Williams, designer; Svetlana Zhurkin, media researcher;
Laura Manthe, production specialist

Photo Credits
Alamy: 19th era, 22, North Wind Picture Archives, cover (middle right), 10; Corbis, 26, Bettmann, 7, 11, National Geographic Society, 9; CriaImages: Jay Robert Nash Collection, 25 (top); DVIC: NARA, 13; Getty Images: Kean Collection, 17; Kansas State Historical Society, 25 (bottom); Library of Congress, cover (bottom left), 5, 14–15, 19, 21, 29; Newscom: KRT/Augustus Washington, 8; Shutterstock: Alena Hovorkova (design elements), throughout, Dianka Pyzhova (design elements), throughout, exshutter (vintage paper sheet), 13, 14, 27, H2O, cover (background), Oleksiy Fedorov (background texture), throughout; Svetlana Zhurkin, 23

Direct Quotes
p. 16 from *To Purge This Land with Blood: A Biography of John Brown* by Stephen B. Oates (New York: Harper & Row, 1970)
p. 17 from *The Life and Letters of Captain John Brown, Who Was Executed at Charlestown, Virginia, Dec. 2, 1859, for an Armed Attack Upon American Slavery, With Notices of Some of his Confederates* edited by Richard Davis Webb (Westport Conn.: Negro Universities Press, 1972)
p. 18 from "John Brown's Day of Reckoning" by Fergus M. Bordewich (Smithsonian Magazine, October 2009)
p. 23 (top) from "Deposition of Edwin Wetmore, November 11, 1859" from The Henry A. Wise Papers in the Library of Congress. 4 March 2013. (http://www.digitalhistory.uh.edu/active_learning/explorations/brown/insane_wetmore.cfm)
p. 23 (bottom) from *John Brown* by Joseph Edgar Chamberlin (Boston: Small, Maynard & Company, 1899)
p. 26 from "Correspondence of The N.Y. Tribune. Petersburg, Va. Nov. 27, 1859." New York Semi-Weekly Tribune, November 29, 1859. 1 March 2013. (http://www.wvculture.org/history/jbexhibit/tribunetrial.html)
p. 27 from *John Brown: A Biography, 1800–1859* by Oswald Garrison Villard (Garden City, N.Y.: Doubleday, Doran & Company, Inc., 1929)

Printed in the United States of America in Brainerd, Minnesota.
032013   007721BANGF13

TABLE OF CONTENTS

The Hanging of John Brown......**4**

Chapter 1
The Making of an Abolitionist...**6**

Chapter 2
First Blood Is Shed............**10**

Chapter 3
The Raid on Harpers Ferry.....**16**

Chapter 4
A Nation Responds............**24**

Chapter 5
History Judges John Brown.....**28**

GLOSSARY......................**30**
READ MORE....................**31**
INTERNET SITES................**31**
CRITICAL THINKING
USING THE COMMON CORE........**31**
INDEX.........................**32**

The Hanging of John Brown

It was a warm morning for December in Charles Town, Virginia, in 1859. Earlier, workers had hammered together **gallows** on the edge of a cornfield. At 11 a.m., soldiers led a thin 60-year-old man up the stairs. He had a long, untidy white beard. He wore a shabby hat and an old dark suit. The soldiers covered his head with a white hood. Then they looped a noose around his neck.

Five long minutes passed. Then 10. Then 15.

Finally the order was given. With one swift motion of his hatchet, the sheriff cut the rope holding the trapdoor. The door fell. The prisoner plunged through the scaffold floor to his death.

The **abolitionist** John Brown—hero to some, villain to others—was dead. But who was this man? Why has he been such a debated topic for more than 150 years?

gallows: a wooden frame used for hanging criminals
abolitionist: a person who worked to end slavery

John Brown climbing the gallows

Chapter 1

THE MAKING OF AN ABOLITIONIST

John Brown was born in Connecticut in 1800. Five years later, his family moved to the wilderness of Ohio. Brown's father, Owen, was a strict, religious man. He was also an abolitionist. Owen believed the Bible said slavery was a sin against God. He taught his children that all people, black and white, were equal.

SLAVERY IN THE UNITED STATES

Buying and selling African slaves was big business. Between 1650 and 1850, 12 million slaves were sold across Africa, the Americas, and Europe. Their children also became slaves.

Slaves were considered property. Owners believed they had the right to punish their slaves. They could be whipped, branded, or beaten.

Slaves first arrived in the North American colonies in 1619. By 1859 there were about 4 million slaves living in the United States. More than 10 percent of the total population was made up of slaves. Most of them worked on farms in the South. More slave labor was used in the southern United States than anywhere in the world.

Throughout his childhood Brown studied the Bible. He came to believe that slavery was an evil that had become a national sin. Getting rid of slavery was the only way to save America from that evil.

Slave families could be split apart and sold to different owners.

7

John Brown in 1847

In 1820 Brown married Dianthe Lusk. She died in 1832. The following year he married 16-year-old Mary Day. Altogether, he had 20 children with his two wives. Over the years Brown opened and closed businesses in four different states. He owned a tannery, raised and traded livestock, and worked as a land **surveyor**. His business travels allowed him to meet others who shared his views against slavery.

When he was 50 years old, Brown and his family moved to North Elba, New York. He allowed his home to be used as a station on the Underground Railroad. It was dangerous, but worth the risk to Brown.

Brown had become a **militant** abolitionist. He believed that God had called on him to stop slavery. If necessary, violence would be used. Blood was a small price to pay to wipe out slavery's sin.

THE UNDERGROUND RAILROAD

The Underground Railroad was a secret network of routes and safe houses. Slaves used this system to escape to the North. People like Brown helped slaves escape. They gave the escaped slaves hiding places, food, transportation, and directions. The network began as early as the 1680s. It grew larger and more effective over the next 150 years. Between 1820 and 1860, about 40,000 slaves used the Underground Railroad.

surveyor: someone who measures areas of land for builders or mapmakers

militant: aggressive or warlike in working toward a cause or ideal

Chapter 2

FIRST BLOOD IS SHED

In 1854 the U.S. Congress passed a law known as the Kansas-Nebraska Act. The new law let people living in those territories decide if slavery would be allowed there. The act angered antislavery people. Slavery had been illegal in Kansas and Nebraska since 1820. The law meant that could change.

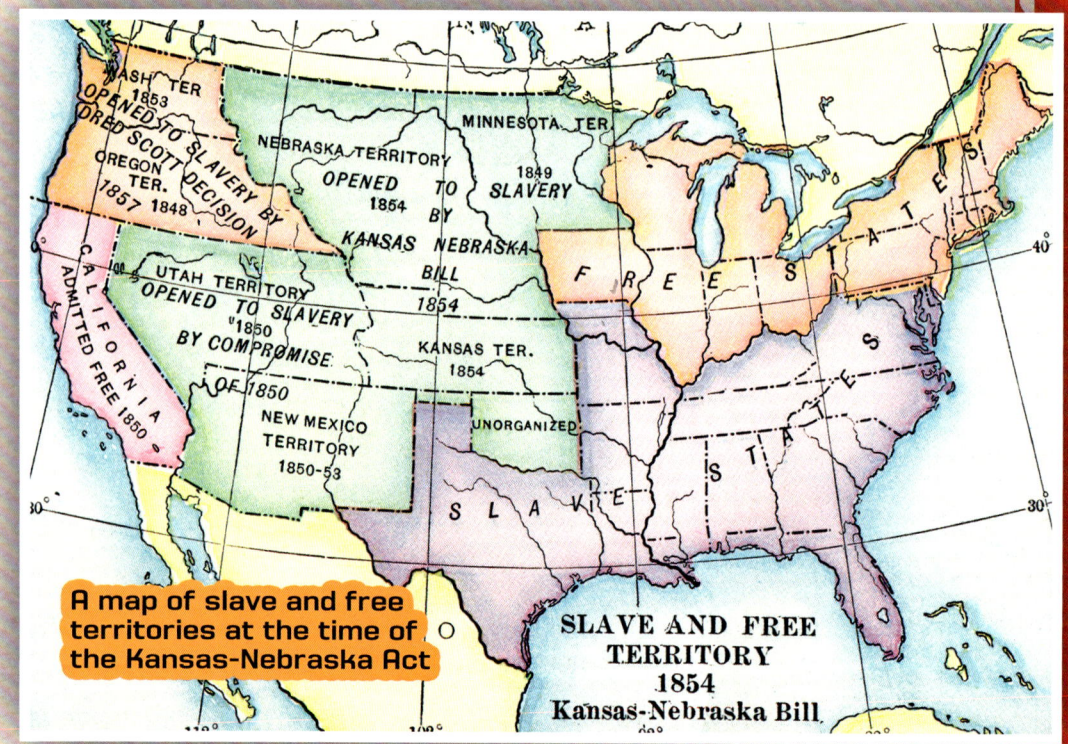

A map of slave and free territories at the time of the Kansas-Nebraska Act

People rushed to the territories. Some people wanted to permanently settle there. Others came to fight for or against slavery. Tensions ran high. Fights broke out often.

Five of Brown's sons moved to Kansas to vote against slavery. In 1855 Brown left his home in New York to join them. Brown saw Kansas as a battlefield of good versus evil. He was prepared to fight those who supported slavery.

A gun fight between abolitionists and slavery supporters in 1850s Kansas

On May 24, 1856, Brown, four of his sons, and several others killed five men at Pottawatomie Creek, Kansas. They believed the men were proslavery. Some people later said Brown was wrong. The event became known as the Pottawatomie **Massacre**.

massacre: the needless killing of a group of helpless people

Brown became a hunted outlaw. If caught and found guilty of the massacre, he could be hanged. He hid in the woods to avoid capture. The killings made Brown the most loved and hated abolitionist in the nation. In the South he was called a madman and a devil. In the North many thought he was a hero.

Brown, now a wanted man, traveled across the North. He spoke about the evils of slavery in churches and meeting halls. He was welcomed as a heroic leader in the fight against slavery. Brown was a good speaker. He convinced many people that slavery was wrong. He raised money for his cause. He even talked some into joining his "army" in Kansas.

In April 1858 Brown gathered a group of followers in Chatham, Canada. There he read his "**Declaration** of Liberty." It was his constitution for a new government. The declaration rejected the idea of slavery. Everyone, black and white, would have equal rights.

declaration: the act of announcing something, or the announcement made

FACT

In December 1858 Brown returned to Kansas with his supporters. While there, they crossed the border into Missouri. They took 11 slaves at gunpoint from two slaveholders. The group killed one slave owner. They also helped themselves to horses and food. After hiding in a farmhouse for a month, Brown helped the slaves escape to Canada.

Brown decided a bold move was the best way to get his message heard. He planned to build an army made up of people of all races. The army would hide in Southern mountains. There, they would be able to help runaway slaves on their journey north. They would also be able to attack slavery supporters. Brown chose an area in Virginia near the small town of Harpers Ferry as his home base.

FACT
Brown's army of 21 men included three of his sons. In July 1859, Brown rented a farmhouse 5 miles (8 kilometers) north of Harpers Ferry. Brown's army lived there. They also used the farmhouse to store guns and ammunition.

Brown and his army planned to attack Harpers Ferry. Their main target was the town's fire engine house. The engine house was property of the U.S. government. It was used as an **arsenal** for army weapons. Brown's army planned to steal all the guns and ammunition they could carry. Then they would flee into the mountains. Brown believed thousands of slaves in the area would join his cause. The weapons from the arsenal would arm them all.

arsenal: a place where weapons are stored

Harpers Ferry lay where the Potomac and Shenandoah Rivers meet.

Chapter 3

THE RAID ON HARPERS FERRY

For two years Brown traveled the country to raise money and soldiers. He intended to attack Harpers Ferry in 1858. However, he changed his plans when he heard one of his men planned to betray him.

By the time Brown was ready to lead the attack, things had changed. Some of his followers had changed their minds and left his army. Others were convinced the plan would no longer work. But Brown was determined to go ahead with the raid.

A STEEL TRAP

In August 1859 Brown told the famous abolitionist Frederick Douglass his plan. Historians believe Douglass did not want Brown to use violence. Douglass also felt that attacking the government was a bad idea. He told Brown, "You're walking into a perfect steel trap, and you will never get out alive."

Brown (left) gathering support near Springfield, Massachusetts

At midnight on October 16, 1859, Brown led 18 men toward Harpers Ferry. A cold rain fell as they marched. They pulled a wagon carrying 200 rifles and 200 pistols. The wagon also held 1,000 **pikes**.

Before they began their march, Brown gave one order. "Consider that the lives of others are as dear to them as yours are to you. Do not, therefore, take the life of anyone, if you can possibly avoid it."

pike: a long, heavy spear

Into Harpers Ferry

Brown's group forced its way into the fire engine house. Brown told the surprised watchmen, "I want to free all the Negroes in this state. If the citizens interfere with me, I must burn the town and have blood."

John Brown's trail from the farmhouse to Harpers Ferry

Today the fire engine house is known as John Brown's Fort.

Brown's men took important white people from the town as **hostages**. He planned to trade them for slaves willing to join his fight. He armed local slaves with pikes to guard the hostages. But to Brown's surprise, no other slaves came to join his army. No one had thought to spread word of the raid to the slave areas farther south.

Brown's men cut the town's telegraph wires. Then they took control of the railroad bridge leading into the town.

hostage: a person held against his or her will

Early in the morning, a train headed into Harpers Ferry was stopped by the townspeople. By then, the local people knew what was happening. They wanted to warn the trainmen.

Three men from the train decided to follow the tracks into town. They wanted to see what was going on. One of the men was Heyward Shepherd, a baggage man on the train. Shepherd saw Brown's gunmen and turned to run. A shot rang out. He fell, wounded, and died later that day. Shepherd, a black man, was the first to die in John Brown's war.

By dawn Harpers Ferry was gripped in terror. Rumors began flying. Some said that thousands of slaves had been freed in the countryside. Slaves were said to be burning houses and killing whites. People believed their greatest fear, a slave **rebellion**, was now happening.

rebellion: a fight against the people in charge

Word of the raid spread. Armed citizens and nearby **militias** swarmed into the area. They began firing on Brown's men. Several people were killed. Soon the militias took control of both bridges leading into town.

Brown shut himself in the fire engine house with several of his soldiers and hostages. The famous abolitionist was trapped.

militia: a group of citizens who are trained to fight, but who only serve in an emergency

This sketch shows the Harpers Ferry battleground. The railroad bridge is on the far left. The fire engine house is on the far right.

Word eventually reached Washington, D.C. President James Buchanan sent backup forces. On the morning of October 18, U.S. soldiers entered the town. Brown's raid on Harpers Ferry was over.

Brown was arrested. He told his captors that he acted to help people who had no one to help them. He came to free them, not to shed blood.

A jury found Brown guilty of murder, **treason**, and organizing a slave rebellion. He was sentenced to hang on December 2. Four of his raiders also shared his fate.

treason: the crime of betraying your country

WAS JOHN BROWN INSANE?

Many people believed John Brown was a crazed madman. A man who knew Brown since childhood said Brown had changed over the years and had become insane. "His whole character seemed changed. He appeared fanatic and furious."

Virginia governor Henry Wise, however, spent hours speaking with Brown after he was captured. Wise later said that Brown was not a madman. He wrote, "[Brown] is a man of clear head ... he has inspired me with great trust in his integrity as a man of truth."

Chapter 4

A NATION RESPONDS

At first most people in the country were outraged at Brown's actions. But in the weeks after his death, opinions in the North changed. American author Henry Thoreau wrote that Brown was a "man of ideas and principles." He praised Brown for his courage to "interfere by force … in order to rescue the slave." The *Boston Daily Advertiser* called Brown a man of "integrity and courage."

Poets and songwriters wrote about his bravery. Church groups held prayer meetings to honor him. William Lloyd Garrison, the abolitionist publisher of the *Liberator*, wrote in Brown's favor. In the North, Brown was spoken of with respect, praise, and admiration. Some did not agree with his use of force at Harpers Ferry. But many saw him as a hero.

REDRAWING HISTORY

There are many ways an artist can redraw history. A battle can be shown as a victory or a loss. A man can be shown as a hero or a villain. Compare these two paintings of John Brown. What do they tell you about the popular opinion of John Brown during the times they were painted?

THE LAST MOMENTS OF JOHN BROWN
by Thomas Hovenden

This etching from 1859 shows Brown's last moments. He is shown kissing a black baby before calmly being led to his execution.

TRAGIC PRELUDE
by John Steuart Curry

This painting done in 1942 shows Brown during the antislavery movement in Kansas. Brown holds a gun and a Bible in his bloody hands. Civil War soldiers fight and die in the background.

25

Southerners were furious at Brown. They saw him as a villain. The invader from the North had come to destroy the Southern way of life.

They were also outraged that the North supported his attack on Virginia. One Southern lawyer said, "I would be glad to see the whole North sunk to the deepest depth of the bottomless pit!"

Brown's trial lasted a little over a week. It was hurried to prevent people from trying to rescue or attack Brown.

John Brown inspired many people into fighting against slavery. His words reached the entire nation. His actions led other people to believe that violence was the right answer. After his raid on Harpers Ferry, Southerners were worried that it might happen again. They formed a militia to protect their farms and families against uprisings. That militia would later become the Confederate Army. That army would fight for slavery in the Civil War (1861–1865).

JOHN BROWN'S FINAL NOTES, WRITTEN ON THE DAY OF HIS HANGING:

"Charlestown, Va, 2nd, December, 1859. I John Brown am now quite certain that the crimes of this guilty, land: will never be purged away; but with Blood. I had as I now think: vainly flattered myself that [without] very much bloodshed; it might be done."

Chapter 5

HISTORY JUDGES JOHN BROWN

Was John Brown a hero or a villain? To this day, opinion is sharply divided. People struggle to understand Brown's actions. Both Harpers Ferry and Pottawatomie had been bloody. Was using violence to fight slavery going too far?

Brown believed he was a soldier in God's army. He was required to perform his duty at all costs.

For years textbooks in the North mentioned Brown's raid as a heroic act. It was written as though it represented the entire antislavery movement. Southern textbooks taught that Brown was a terrorist. He had come to the South to murder innocent white citizens. He had been behind one of the worst crimes in American history.

There are no simple answers to who John Brown truly was. The images of Brown as saint or madman have faded. Scholars now hold more complex views of him. Yet Brown continues to spark debate. His actions make people question their own beliefs and examine their way of life.

GLOSSARY

abolitionist (ab-uh-LI-shuhn-ist)—a person who worked to end slavery

arsenal (AR-suh-nuhl)—a place where weapons and ammunitions are made or stored

declaration (dek-luh-RAY-shuhn)—the act of announcing something, or the announcement made

gallows (GAL-ohz)—a wooden frame used for hanging criminals

hostage (HOSS-tij)—a person held against his or her will

massacre (MASS-uh-kuhr)—the needless killing of a group of helpless people

militant (MIL-uh-tuhnt)—aggressive or warlike in pursuing some cause or ideal

militia (muh-LISH-uh)—a group of citizens who are trained to fight, but who only serve in an emergency

pike (PIKE)—a long, heavy spear

rebellion (ri-BEL-yuhn)—a fight against the people in charge

surveyor (suhr-VAY-uhr)—someone who measures areas of land for builders or mapmakers

treason (TREE-zuhn)—the crime of betraying your country

READ MORE

Burgan, Michael. *African Americans in the Thirteen Colonies.* Cornerstones of Freedom. New York: Children's Press, 2013.

Fradin, Judith Bloom. *The Price of Freedom: How One Town Stood Up to Slavery.* New York: Walker & Co., 2013.

Glaser, Jason. *John Brown's Raid on Harpers Ferry.* Graphic History. Mankato, Minn.: Capstone Press, 2006.

INTERNET SITES

FactHound offers a safe, fun way to find Internet sites related to this book. All of the sites on FactHound have been researched by our staff.

Here's all you do:
Visit *www.facthound.com*
Type in this code: 9781476502441

Check out projects, games and lots more at www.capstonekids.com

CRITICAL THINKING USING THE COMMON CORE

1. Brown was not afraid to use violence in order to free slaves. Do you think he was justified in his reasoning? Why or why not? (Key Ideas and Details)

2. Examine the two paintings on page 25. How do they impact your view of Brown? Which do you think is more believable? Support your answer with details from the text. (Craft and Structure)

3. The author states that Brown was the most loved and most hated abolitionist in the country. What do you think this means? (Integration of Knowledge and Ideas)

INDEX

Brown, John
  army of, 12, 14, 16, 19
  arrest of, 23
  birth of, 6
  children of, 8, 11, 14
  execution of, 4, 5, 25, 27
  in art, 25
  jobs of, 8
  trial of, 23, 26
  wives of, 8
Brown, Owen (father), 6
Buchanan, James, 23

Charles Town, Virginia, 4

"Declaration of Liberty," 12
Douglass, Frederick, 16

Garrison, William Lloyd, 24

Harpers Ferry, 14, 15, 16, 17, 18, 20, 21, 23, 24, 27, 28
  fire engine house, 15, 18, 19, 21, 23

Kansas-Nebraska Act, 10

Pottawatomie Massacre, 11, 12, 28

Shepard, Hayward, 20

Thoreau, Henry, 24

Underground Railroad, 8, 9

Wise, Henry, 23